ABOUT BEADS

The beads we use for the stitches in this book can be purchased just about anywhere in the world. They include glass beads, mainly seed, bugle and Delica (cylindrical) beads. Also used are pearl beads and sequins, which you really need for floral designs.

Seed beads

Though the sizes of these tiny round beads most often used are 2mm and 3mm, smaller and larger seed beads are also available.

Bugle beads

These long, narrow cylinders are sold in lengths ranging from 1.5mm to 30mm. They are available with both smooth and twisted surfaces.

Pearl beads

The basic pearl bead is round, but you can also find oval shapes the size of rice grains, and teardrop beads. They come in gold, silver and other colors, in addition to white.

Delica beads

Delicas are tiny cylindrical beads originally intended for loom weaving. They come in two sizes: 1.6mm and 3mm. Their large holes distinguish Delicas from other beads of this type.

Triangle beads (purple)

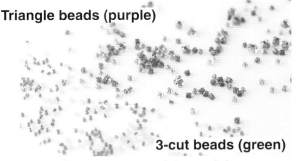

3-cut beads (green)

Beads come in a multitude of sizes and shapes. Shown above are triangle beads and 3-cut beads, which have irregular cuts on their surfaces.

Sequins

Sequins are small metal discs. They are available in an amazing range of shapes and styles (stars and flowers, just to name a few). Some have holes at their edges. They add sparkle to bead embroidery.
But they are sensitive to heat and humidity, so don't wash or iron sequin embroidery.

All the beads used for the projects in this book are made by Miyuki Co.

TOOLS AND SUPPLIES

You'll need the tools and supplies shown on these pages for bead embroidery. Good tools make your work easier and help you create beautiful embroidery. None of these items is expensive, so plan on purchasing them a few at a time.

First things first: Must-have items

1. Beads

Beads are usually packaged in plastic envelopes or tubes and sold by weight (generally gram weight). Ask your supplier to estimate the number of beads in a package if you can't tell. You'll be using tiny beads, which can easily spill or get lost, so it's a good idea to buy more than you think you'll need. Sometimes you can find color mixtures in one package.

1. Packaged Miyuki beads
2. Bead embroidery needles (these are made by Clover)
3. DMC embroidery floss

Storing beads
You can always keep your beads in the packages they came in. Other convenient options are transparent cases and reclosable plastic bags. Write the product number and size of each type of bead on a label, and affix it to the case or bag.

Picking up beads
When you embroider with beads, you pick the beads up one by one with your needle. Placing the beads in a paper plate makes this process much easier.

3. Needles

There are beading needles designed especially for bead embroidery. They are longer and thinner than ordinary needles to accommodate multiple, tiny beads. We also use very fine Japanese sewing needles, but these are not available outside Japan at this time. You may find that ordinary sewing needles will work just fine.

Left to right: Beading needle, very fine Japanese sewing needles

Needle-threaders
These handy devices are available in many styles, from the simple to the ornate. Don't use them with beading needles, though, because those needles are delicate and may break. The needle-threader shown here is made by Clover.

2. Embroidery floss

You will be working with one doubled strand of #25 floss (thread needle with one strand, then join the ends with a knot). Generally, you will use thread in the same color family as the beads you are using, or thread that matches your foundation fabric. But there will be exceptions; for instance, you can get create wonderful effects using colored thread with transparent beads.

Working with embroidery floss

Place thread inside the wire loop of the needle-threader, insert the loop into the hole in the needle, and pull.

The threads in a skein of floss are 8m long. You can cut 1m at a time, or cut the skein into eight equal lengths before you begin. Attach a label to the thread so you'll always know the color number.

Embroidery floss comes in skeins of six strands. You will be using one strand. Hold the skein in one hand, and pull one thread out of it with the other.

Embroidery scissors and pincushion
It's a good idea to have small embroidery scissors on hand for cutting thread, and a pincushion.

Embroidery scissors, pincushion (Clover)

4. Fabric

Because of the highly decorative nature of bead embroidery, luxury fabrics like satin, silk shantung, moiré, velvet and velveteen are best because you want something that will complement your embroidery. Other possibilities are knits, linen and linen blends. Avoid shaggy fabrics that might snag, and loosely woven fabrics that can't support the beads. Thin, gauzy fabrics like organdy and chiffon are sometimes used, but they are hard to work with; sturdier fabrics are best for beginners.

Tools you'll need to transfer patterns

1. Tracing paper
2. Chacopy (transfer paper)
3. Water-erasable marking pen
4. Stylus
5. Straight pins
6. Cellophane

1. Tracing paper
Use this to transfer designs.

2. Chacopy (transfer paper)
Used in the same way as tracing paper, but has chalk on one surface. Choose a brand that comes with an erasing pen or is water-soluble.

3. Water-erasable marking pen
Use this type of pen when you are adding to a transferred pattern or drawing freehand on fabric. Make sure that the pen has a fine point that draws clear lines, and that the "ink" is water-soluble.

4. Stylus
Transfer your design with a stylus when you use Chacopy.You can also use a pencil with a hard lead (2H or harder) or a ballpoint pen that's run out of ink.

5. Straight pins
Use these to secure your pattern to fabric.

6. Cellophane
Place a sheet of cellophane on top of the tracing paper, then trace your pattern with a stylus. The cellophane will keep the pattern from tearing, so you'll be able to use it again and again.

Transferring a pattern

Place the tracing paper with the pattern on it on top of the fabric. Secure paper to fabric with straight pins at the top. Place transfer paper between the two layers, and then a sheet of cellophane on top. Trace the pattern with a stylus.

Remove the transfer paper to see the pattern on the fabric.

Removing a pattern element

Use an erasing pen or a cotton swab moistened with water.

Finishing tools

When you use a flexible ironing mat (the one in the photograph is 100% cotton), you get really good results because the mat "absorbs" the beads. With the wrong side up, grasp the fabric with your left hand and let the iron smooth out the fabric that got wrinkled while you were embroidering. If your piece includes sequins, which tend to melt when exposed to heat, be sure that the iron doesn't touch them.

Embroidery hoops
Use a hoop when you need the fabric to be taut, for instance, when you're doing couching.

Before you begin ...

You're probably thinking, "How did I get into this? I have no idea what I'm doing."
Well, don't worry. Once you learn a few basic techniques,
you'll find that bead embroidery is quite easy (and fun).

Beads and stitches

● The names of the stitches that appear in this book are the same as those in conventional thread embroidery. The only difference is that with bead embroidery, you will be stringing beads on the thread.

● When you make line stitches, a good gauge is 5-7 (8mm-15mm) beads on one stitch, depending, of course, on the size of beads you are using. When you use more beads than that, they tend to sag. (The lazy daisy stitch is an exception to this rule.)

Finishing off thread

This is done by forming a knot to secure your embroidery firmly to the fabric.

Note: In the photos we often show all 12 strands of floss, or thicker thread, for clarity's sake.

But when you embroider, you'll be using one strand of floss, doubled.

  * Feel free to use another knot or method, as long as it secures the thread.

Beginning knot *

Grasp the end of the thread and wind it once around your index finger.

Twist thread between your thumb and index finger several times.

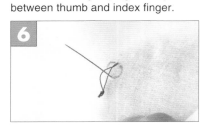

Pull on thread, grasping it firmly between thumb and index finger.

You have formed a knot at the end of the thread.

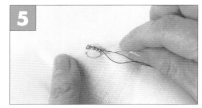

Pass needle through fabric to wrong side. Insert needle between the two strands of thread.

Pull on thread to secure your knot.

This is how the right side of the fabric looks when you've inserted the needle through it from the wrong side and are about to complete your first stitch. To anchor beads securely to fabric, pass the needle between the two threads.

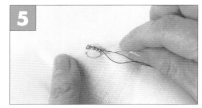

Make sure you have enough thread (you will need thread that is twice as long as the needle). Bring needle out on wrong side of fabric and align it with the thread.

Ending knot *

Make this knot when you run out of thread or come to a stopping point.

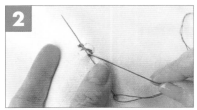

Wrap thread around needle two or three times; pull wound thread down toward fabric.

Press down on thread wound around needle with your left thumb, and pull the needle upwards.

Run needle under a stitch two or three times; cut thread.

Moving to another location without cutting the thread

First, make an ending knot. Then run the needle under stitches, bringing it out at the next location. (If you move directly to another location, leaving a long bridge thread, other threads may get caught in it, causing your embroidery to pucker.)

If the new location is more than 3cm away, just make a knot and move there. If it is farther away than that, make an ending knot, cut the thread.

Removing the needle when you've inserted it incorrectly

You've inserted your needle into the wrong place.

Pull the fabric outward with both hands until it is taut. Keeping the fabric taut and the needle vertical, pull on the thread from the wrong side with your fingers. The needle should slip through the fabric to the wrong side.

Embroidering on knit fabric

Knits and some other fabrics are not suited to transferring patterns. When you embroider on such fabrics, use thin Japanese paper *(washi)*, which can be removed after your embroidery is completed.

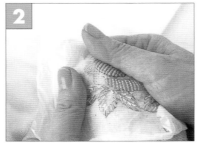

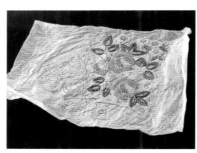

Transfer your pattern onto the Japanese paper. Rub the paper between your hands to soften it so it won't tear. Pin the paper to the knit fabric, then baste around edges with one strand #25 DMC embroidery floss. Remove pins.

When you've finished embroidering, remove the basting. Holding onto the beads with one hand, tear the paper off, a little at a time, with the other.

Finished embroidery

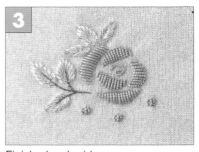

Use this same method with the Japanese paper when you embroider on velvet, velveteen and other fabrics with a nap.

1. Line Stitches

Two examples of line stitches are the outline stitch, which involves working backwards 1/3 of the way into a "line" and then moving forward again; and the couching stitch, where you anchor long lines with small stitches.

These are the first two stitches we'll learn. Simply follow the lines of your pattern, pulling on the thread as you go to keep the tension taut.

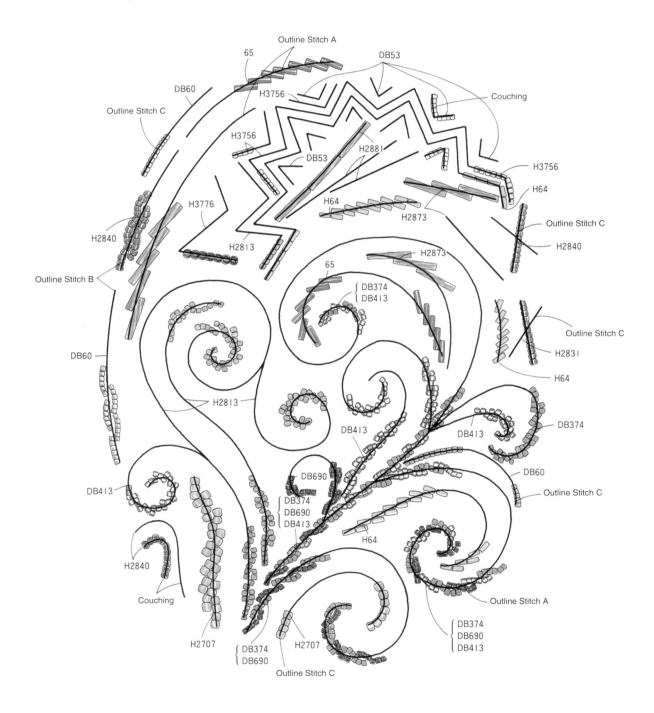

(Stitches in photo above are actual size.)

Supplies
2-mm seed beads: H2831, H2840, H3756
3-mm seed beads: H3776
1.6-mm Delica beads: DB53, DB60, DB374, DB413, DB690
Bugle beads: H64 (3mm), H65 (6mm), H2873, H2881 (12mm)
2.2-mm 3-cut beads: H2813
3-mm triangle beads: H2707

Outline Stitch A

Place each stitch on the same side of the previous stitch (top or bottom).

Outline Stitch B

Alternate between top and bottom of previous stitch.

(Stitches in samplers are actual size.)

Outline Stitch A

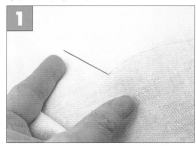

Bring needle out on right side of fabric. If you're making a spiral, start from the inside.

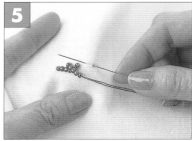

Pick up same number of beads and repeat Steps 3-4.

Outline Stitch B

You make this stitch the same way as Outline Stitch A, with one exception. When you work backwards 1/3 of the way, you bring the needle with the beads on it out above or below the stitch, alternating between the two directions. First you'll be placing the yellow-green beads 1/3 of the way back below the stitch.

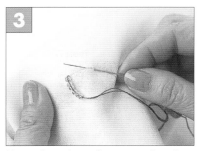

Next, place the yellow-green beads below the previous stitch.

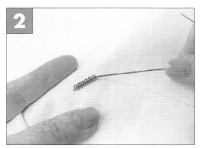

Pick up 6 beads at a time (if you're using 2-mm seed beads), following the lines of your traced pattern.

Insert needle into fabric, pointed toward beginning of work, and bring it out 1/3 of the way back from end of stitch (the distance covered by 2 beads).

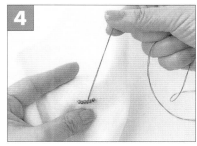

Pull on thread.

After you've made a few stitches, you'll see that the beads are forming a line in the shape of a backwards "S".

Tip

To make this stitch, you reverse your direction, going back 1/3 of the way and then moving ahead. When you go backwards, you should always bring your needle out above the beads (or below them, depending on the decision you made before you began). The stitches in the sample on p. 8 show the beads forming a gently curved S.

Tips

Place the green beads above the previous stitch.

Outline Stitch A

Outline Stitch B

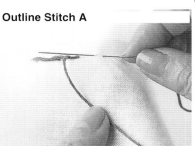

Check your work against the stitches (sewn without beads) in the photographs above to make sure your stitches are correct.

Always insert your needle into and bring it out on the lines in your pattern.

Keep the fabric taut by holding it between your left thumb and index finger as you work. If you follow this rule, even without a hoop, you will get good results and the beads won't sag.

Continue working in the same way, alternating between top and bottom of stitches.

Outline Stitch C

Forms a continuous line.

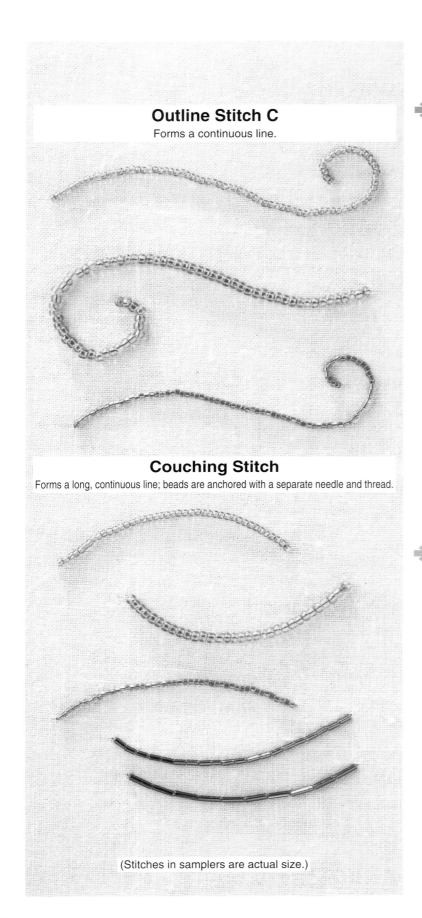

Couching Stitch

Forms a long, continuous line; beads are anchored with a separate needle and thread.

(Stitches in samplers are actual size.)

Outline Stitch C

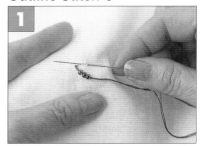

1

Pick up 3 beads, then bring needle out 2/3 of the way back toward starting point (the length of 2 beads).

4

Remember to pull thread after each repetition.

Couching Stitch

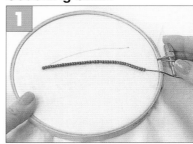

1

Pick up enough beads to cover the line on your pattern. With couching, it's better to use a hoop because it keeps the fabric taut and makes it easier to embroider.

5

Repeat Steps 3 and 4 every three beads.

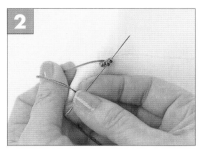

Pass needle through the second and third beads added in Step 1; pull thread.

Repeat Steps 1 and 2.

After you've made a few stitches, you'll notice that the beads form a straight line when you pull the thread in the direction you're working.

Tip

Outline Stitch C is best for shorter lines and spirals. Use the couching stitch for longer lines.

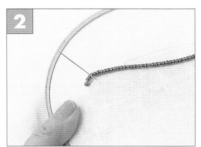

Using a separate needle and thread, anchor 2 or 3 beads at a time. First, bring your needle out at the third or fourth bead from beginning of work on the line in your pattern.

Insert needle into fabric across line of beads.

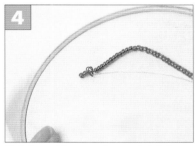

Pull thread from underneath fabric, making sure you brought needle out at and inserted it into the right places.

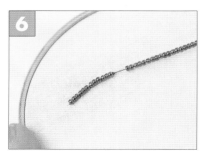

If the beads have fallen out of line, pull the thread to straighten them.

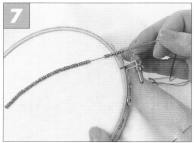

When you reach the end of the line on your pattern, make a knot on the wrong side of fabric. Remove any extra beads.

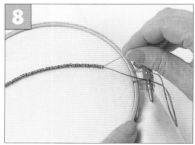

Make a knot on wrong side of fabric with thread holding the beads.

2. Filling stitches

The important thing to remember about this type of stitch is direction.
When you're stitching a curve, the stitches should be closer together on the inside
and farther apart on the outside.

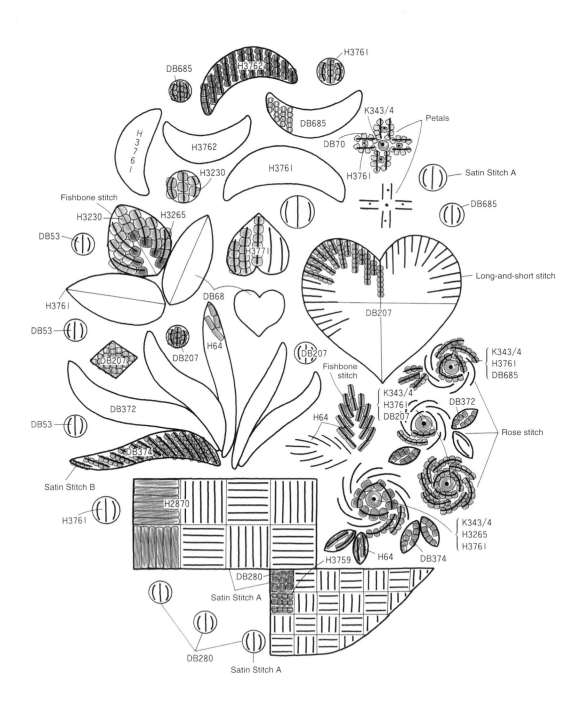

(Stitches in photo above are actual size.)

Supplies
2-mm seed beads: H3759, H3761, H3762
3-mm seed beads: H3771
1.6-mm Delica beads: DB53, DB60, DB70, DB207, DB280, DB372, DB374, DB685
12-mm bugle beads: H64, H2870
3-mm triangle beads: H3230, H3265
4-mm pearl beads (gold): K343/4

Satin Stitch A
Straight stitch used to fill a space

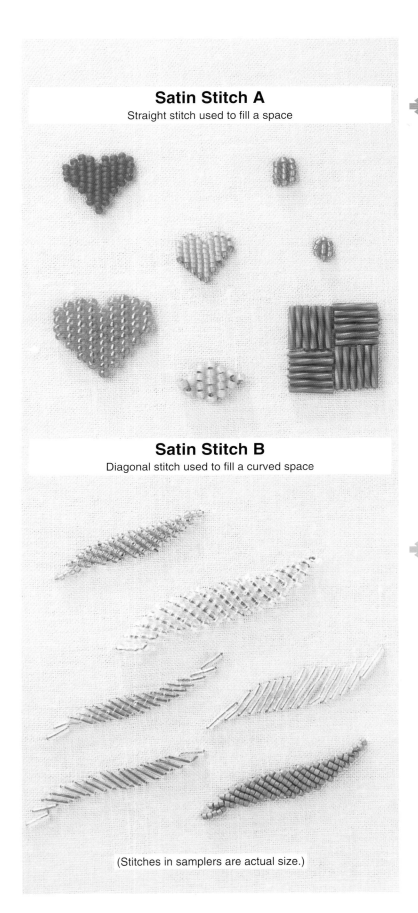

Satin Stitch B
Diagonal stitch used to fill a curved space

(Stitches in samplers are actual size.)

Satin Stitch A

1

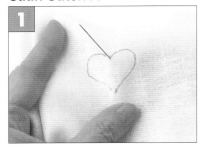

Begin embroidering at center of pattern.

5

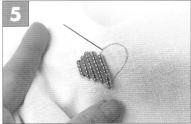

When you've finished embroidering one side of the pattern, make a knot on the wrong side (see Steps 5-7 of the long-and-short stitch on p. 17). Bring needle out on other side of design.

Satin Stitch B

1

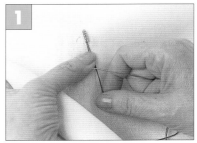

Begin at the inner curve (where the distance covered by the curve is shortest). Bring needle out at the peak of the pattern.

3

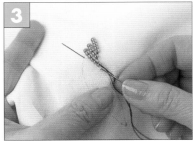

Always insert needle into and bring it out on the lines in the pattern.

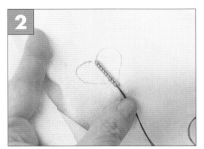

String beads until they cover center of pattern.

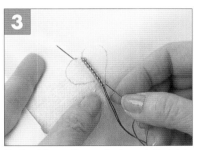

Embroider patterns that are left-right mirror-image one half at a time. Gauge the location of your next stitch according to the width of the beads.

Secure the beads by inserting the needle between the two threads on each stitch.

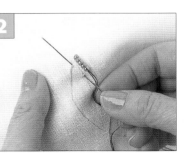

Embroider other side of design, being sure to use the same number of beads. (When you are working in mirror image, use the same number of beads on both sides.)

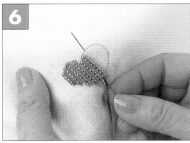

Begin your next stitch, taking the width of the beads into account.

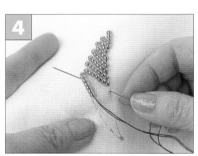

Stitches should be close together on the inner curve and farther apart on the outer curve.

Tips

Selecting colors when using transparent or translucent beads

The colors of the floss (shown at left and right in photographs) are muted by the beads. If you think the color you've selected is a little too dark, it's probably just right.

Gauging the number of beads to your design

When we embroider, we adjust the number of beads according to the lines in the pattern we're following. There will be times when you think you should add just one more bead, others when you think you should perhaps subtract one bead. In cases like this, it's best to opt for fewer beads.

Long-and-Short Stitch

Just as its name implies, this stitch is made by alternating long stitches with short ones. It is ideal for large areas and wide curves.

Fishbone Stitch

This stitch, which forms a V, is used for left-right mirror-image shapes.

(Stitches in samplers are actual size.)

Long-and-short Stitch

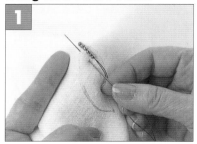

1

Embroider one side at a time.

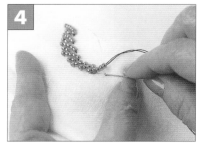

4

Once you've finished one side, bring needle out on wrong side of fabric.

8

Bring needle out at starting point for other side of design.

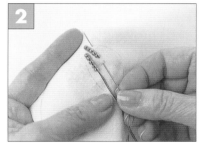

2

With this stitch, you work both sides at the same time. Bring needle out at the same location on opposite side of pattern.

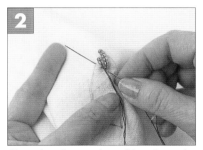

Changing the number of beads each time, make one long stitch, then one short stitch. Repeat.

The short stitches make it easier to change the angle of the next long stitch. They also make it easy to form sharp outer curves. Remember that there's nothing sacred about the progression (long, short, long, short), either. If you need an extra short stitch to form an angle properly, go ahead and add it. Above all, follow your pattern exactly.

Insert the eye end of the needle under your stitches, one at a time, and pull up to tighten the thread.

Make an ending knot.

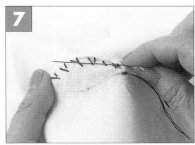

Run needle under the stitches until you arrive at the starting point. (When you are making filling stitches, always follow Steps 5-7 when you finish one side of your pattern.)

Repeat the stitch pattern (long, short, long, etc.) on the other side.

Fishbone Stitch

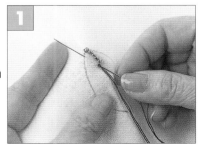

Begin at the center, then bring your needle out at the top of the next stitch.

Repeat, working from left to right, then left to right again.

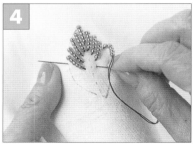

Stitches should be closer together on the inside than on the outside.

Bring needle out on wrong side of fabric. Make an ending knot.

Begin by stitching a central triangle.

Rose Stitch

Similar to the outline stitch, this stitch is used to form a rose.

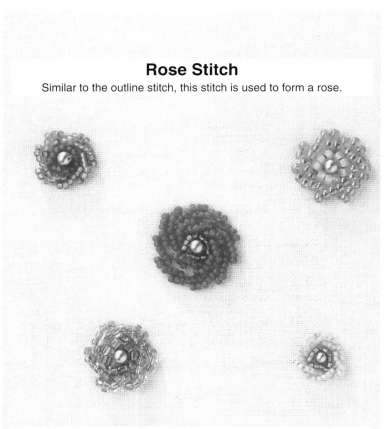

Repeat, working counterclockwise.

Petal Stitch

This stitch is made by forming two parallel lines of beads and inserting a bead between them to form a petal.

(Stitches in samplers are actual size.)

Repeat Step 6.

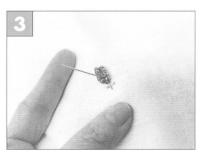

Bring needle out between the two lines of beads.

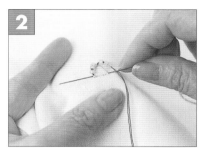
Form a triangle, using the same number of beads on all three sides.

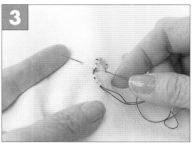
Bring needle out at top of triangle (the first edge you stitched becomes the bottom).

Pick up 6 beads. Working the outline stitch, make curves around the central triangle.

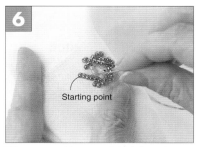
When round is completed, insert needle 2 or 3 beads away from starting point.

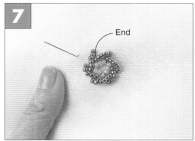
If you're going to embroider another round, begin at the top of the triangle.

Continue as if working outline stitch.

Petal Stitch

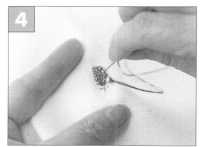
For a nice effect, use a slightly larger pearl bead for the center of the flower.

Make a petal by creating two parallel lines. Leave a little bit of space at the center (insert the needle slightly toward the left).

The second line of beads goes right next to the first one.

When you insert the needle into the larger bead at the center, the two lines of beads will form a curve around the larger bead.

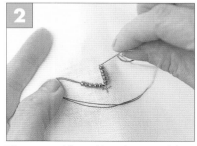
Depending on the number of petals, embroider them in this order: vertical, horizontal (if any), diagonal (if any).

Add a pearl bead at center of flower.

3. Looped stitches

Two basic stitches in this family are the lazy daisy stitch (also called the detached chain stitch), which forms loops. and the fly stitch, which forms a Y.
Both offer limitless possibilities. One of the many appealing aspects of bead embroidery is the freedom to combine beads of different colors and sizes.
Feel free to mix colors and to combine large and small beads.

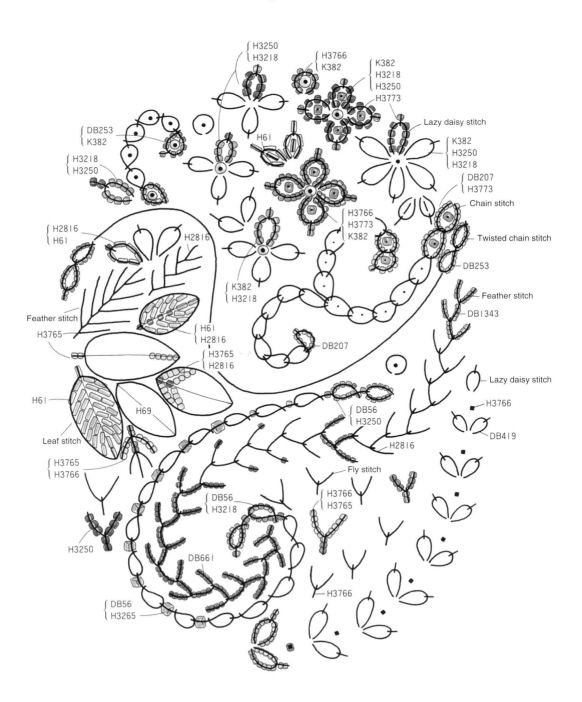

(Stitches in photo are actual size.)

Supplies
2-mm seed beads: H3765, H3766
3-mm seed beads: H3773
1.6-mm Delica beads: DB56, DB207, DB253, DB419, DB661, DB1343
Bugle beads: H61 (3mm), H69 (6mm)
Triangle beads: H3218, H3250 (2.5mm), H3265 (3mm)
2.2-mm 3-cut beads: H2816
2.5-mm pearl beads: K382

Lazy Daisy Stitch

Forms an anchored loop.

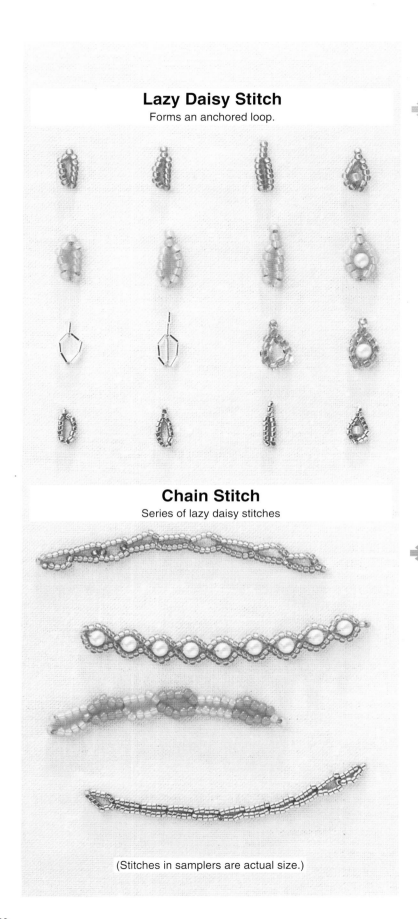

Chain Stitch

Series of lazy daisy stitches

(Stitches in samplers are actual size.)

1

Bring needle out on right side of fabric at top of loop.

Chain Stitch

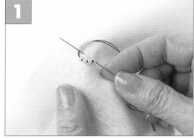

1

Work Steps 1-3 of the lazy daisy stitch.

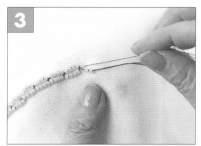

3

As you did at the end of the lazy daisy stitch, add 2 more beads, then bring needle out on wrong side of fabric and make a knot.

5

Repeat Steps 1-4. This stitch goes quickly when you insert the needle and bring it out in the same movement.

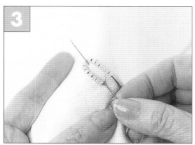

Pick up enough beads to cover entire loop; return to starting point.

Insert needle just to the right of starting point. Bring needle out at top center and pull thread.

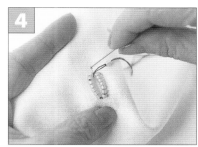

Add 2 more beads, bring needle out on wrong side of fabric, and make a knot.

Pick up the same number of beads, then insert needle to the right of the thread extending from fabric. Bring needle out on the line on your pattern.

Without cutting the thread, bring the needle out on right side of fabric. Pick up a pearl bead. Insert needle next to thread extending from fabric to secure pearl bead.

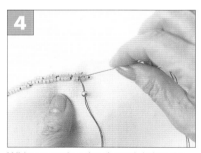

The pearl beads add volume to your chain.

Tips

Lazy daisy stitch combinations

You can create a variety of shapes by forming lazy daisy stitch combinations, working from the center out. For instance, four stitches form a flower, three a crown, and two a leaf.

When you are combining an even number of stitches, the order should be (working from the center) vertical stitches, horizontal stitches (if any) and diagonal stitches (if any).

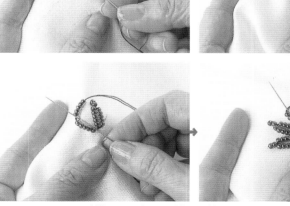

When you're working with an odd number of stitches, make the center stitch first.

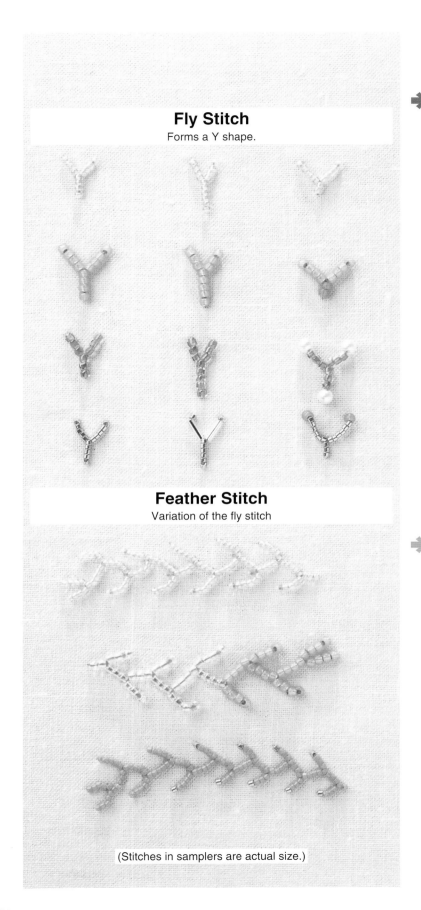

Fly Stitch
Forms a Y shape.

Feather Stitch
Variation of the fly stitch

(Stitches in samplers are actual size.)

Fly Stitch

First, make the V portion of the Y. Pick up an even number of beads, enough to cover the V.

Adding accent beads to the fly stitch

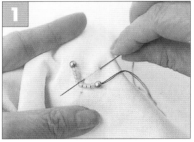

Add contrasting beads to the points of the Y for a dramatic effect.

Feather Stitch

This is similar to the fly stitch, except that you work in the opposite direction. Pick up an even number of beads, form a V, and bring the needle out a slight distance away from the guideline on your pattern.

As the lines lengthen, increase the number of beads.

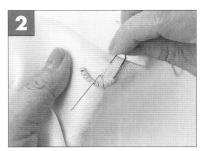

Keeping the beads below the needle, insert the needle into the fabric at right side of the V and bring it out at the bottom of the V.

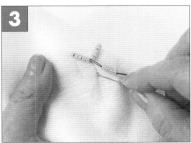

Pull on the thread until each side of the V has the same number of beads on it. Anchor the V by adding more beads and inserting needle into the bottom of the Y.

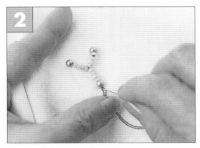

The stitch is made in the same way as usual.

Feather stitch used as a filling stitch

Make another V on opposite side of the guideline, using the same number of beads,

Repeat Steps 1 and 2.

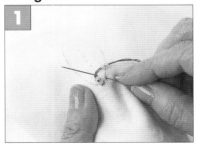

Make feather stitch as usual, starting at the apex of the guideline in your pattern.

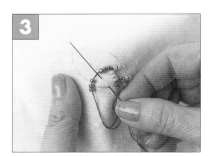

If you are working in left-right mirror image and adding, for instance, 6 beads on the right side, add the same number of beads on the left side.

When forming the V, you don't need to have the same number of beads on the left and right sides.

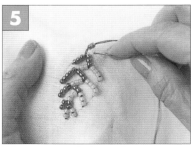

When you reach the end, you can add more beads (here, two), or you can end the stitch without adding beads.

Twisted Chain Stitch

The twisted look comes from reinserting the needle to one side of the previous stitch.

Leaf Stitch

Formed by joining fly stitches to make a leaf shape

(Stitches in samplers are actual size.)

1

Begin in the same way as regular chain stitch.

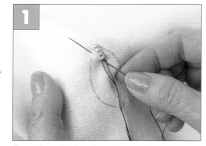

5

Insert beads into the center of the loops for a garland effect.

Leaf Stitch

1

Start by placing beads at the center of the leaf. Bring needle out at beginning of next stitch, taking size of beads into account.

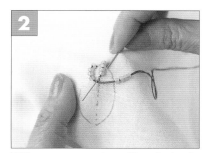

2

With an even number of beads, begin working the fly stitch, dividing beads in half at center of stitch.

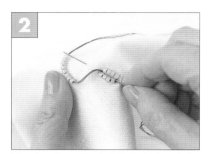

Here's where the twisted chain stitch differs from the chain stitch. Insert your needle into fabric outside (not inside) the loop.

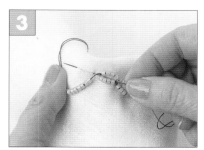

Repeat Steps 1 and 2. Insert needle into fabric outside the loop, bring it out on the guideline, and pull the thread.

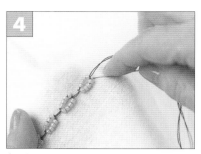

As the distance between the insertion point and the loop grows, the thread will begin showing on the right side of the fabric.

Tip

Work the chain and twisted chain stitches without beads to make sure you're not confusing the two.

Chain stitch

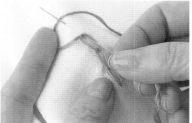

To make the chain stitch, you insert the needle from the inside of the loop directly to the right of the thread extending from the fabric.

Twisted chain stitch

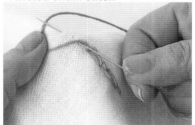

For the twisted chain stitch, you insert the needle from outside the loop into the top of the guideline on the pattern.

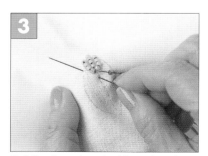

Pull the thread and add one bead. Insert needle into center line and bring it out at starting point for next stitch.

Repeat these steps, increasing the number of beads as the leaf widens.

Completed leaf with a vein in the center

4. Detached Stitches

Use these stitches when you want to create a random pattern (a starlit sky, for instance) or when you want to add one or two beads to an empty space.
For best results, pull the thread in the direction you're working in after each stitch.

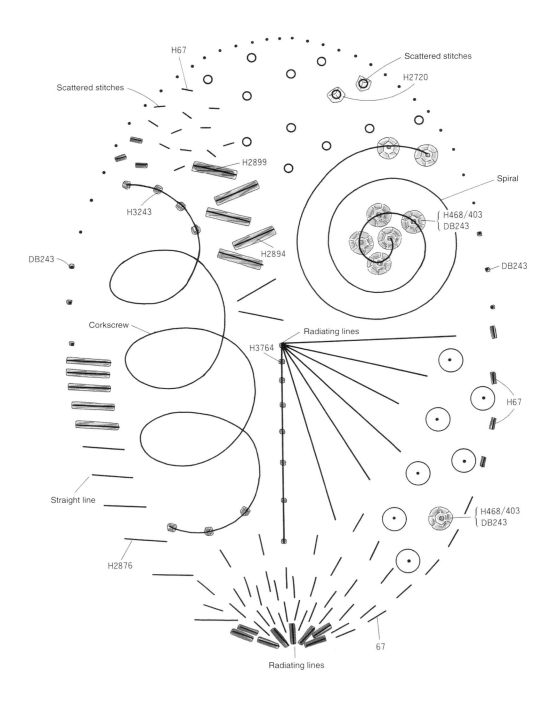

Scattered stitches
H67
Scattered stitches
H2720
H2899
H3243
H2894
DB243
DB243
Spiral
H468/403
DB243
DB243
Corkscrew
Radiating lines
H3764
H67
H468/403
DB243
Straight line
H2876
67
Radiating lines

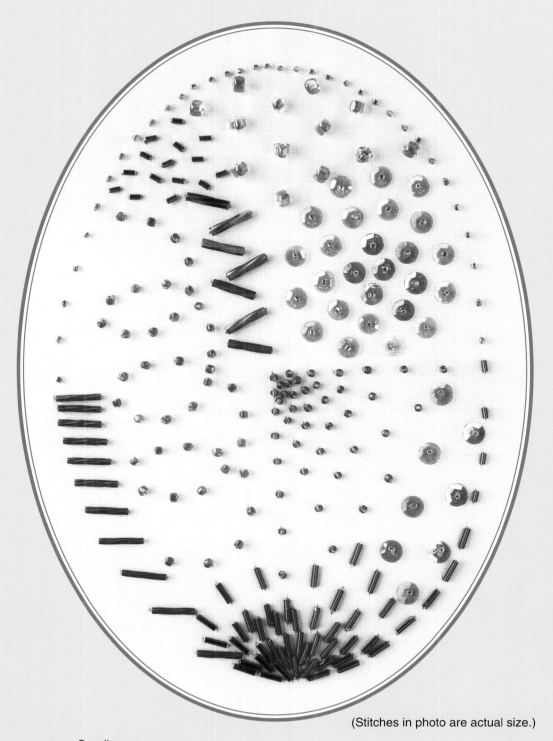

(Stitches in photo are actual size.)

Supplies
2-mm seed beads: H3764
1.6-mm Delica beads: DB243
Bugle beads: H67 (3mm), H67 (6mm), H2876, H2894, H2899 (12mm)
Triangle beads: H2720 (5mm), H3243 (2.5mm)
6-mm cup sequins: H468/403

Scattered stitches
Stitches that anchor single beads

Straight stitches
Backstitches that anchor lines of beads

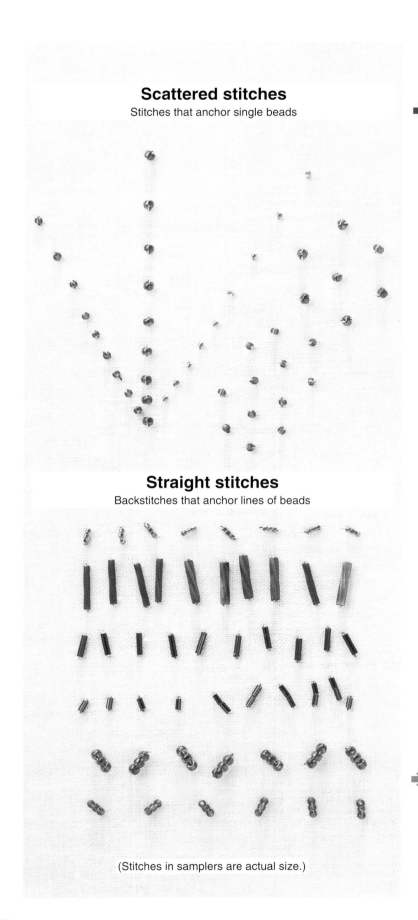

(Stitches in samplers are actual size.)

Radiating lines

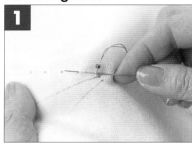

Bring needle through fabric to right side. String bead on thread, then insert needle into fabric just to the right of the bead and bring it out at location of next stitch.

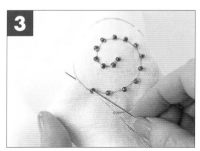

We call this stitch, which involves stitching backwards and then forward, the "backstitch."

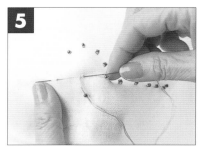

For a really beautiful spiral, increase the amount of space between beads gradually.

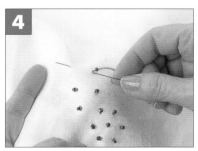

Consider increasing the size of the triangles as you go along.

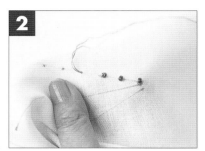

2

After you've made a few stitches, the holes in the beads tend to end up facing upwards.

3

To correct this problem, pull the thread toward the next stitch (the stitch you're about to make).

4

Bring needle out on wrong side of fabric and make a knot.

6

Stitching beads onto fabric diagonally, with the guideline at center, creates an interesting effect.

Spirals

1

Spirals are worked from the center out.

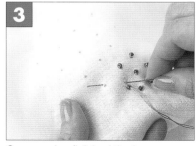

2

Anchor the beads by backstitching.

Scattered stitches

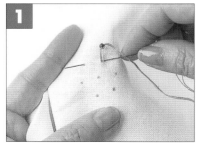

1

Begin with a hexagon with a center.

2

Keep in mind at all times that you are making a triangle.

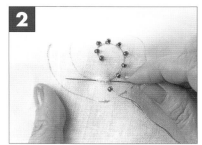

3

Once you've finished the hexagon, proceed to the next triangle.

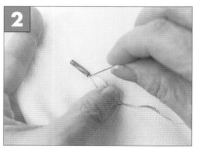

5

If you keep making triangles, your work will have a nice balance.

Straight stitches

1

The main thing to remember here is to insert the needle between the two strands of floss.

2

The technique is the same, whether you're attaching one bead or several beads. You anchor each addition with a backstitch.

5. Variations

When you add sequins to the equation, you'll discover a multitude of variations. You'll find yourself entering a world of wonderful new stitches when you use or combine the stitches we've introduced in this book.

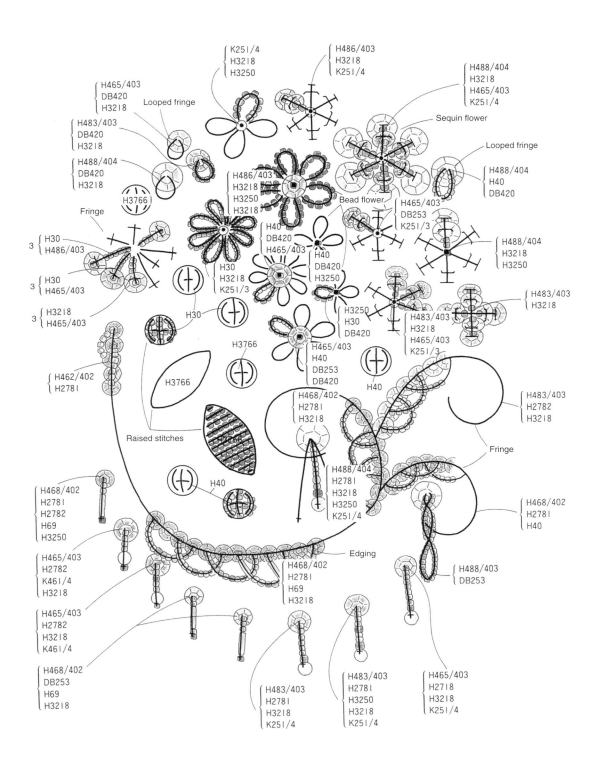

K251/4
H3218
H3250

H486/403
H3218
K251/4

H488/404
H3218
H465/403
K251/4

Sequin flower

H465/403
DB420
H3218

Looped fringe

H483/403
DB420
H3218

H488/404
DB420
H3218

H3766

Fringe

H486/403
H3218
H3250
H3218

Bead flower

Looped fringe

H488/404
H40
DB420

H465/403
DB253
K251/3

H488/404
H3218
H3250

3 { H30
   H486/403

3 { H30
   H465/403

3 { H3218
   H465/403

H40
DB420
H465/403

H40
DB420
H3250

H30
H3218
K251/3

H30

H483/403
H3218
H465/403
K251/3

H483/403
H3218

H3250
H30
DB420

H3766

H3766

H465/403
H40
DB253
DB420

H40

H462/402
H2781

H468/402
H2781
H3218

H483/403
H2782
H3218

Fringe

Raised stitches

H40

H488/404
H2781
H3218
H3250
K251/4

H468/402
H2781
H40

H468/402
H2781
H2782
H69
H3250

H465/403
H2782
K461/4
H3218

Edging

H468/402
H2781
H69
H3218

H488/403
DB253

H465/403
H2782
H3218
K461/4

H468/402
DB253
H69
H3218

H483/403
H2781
H3218
K251/4

H483/403
H2781
H3250
H3218
K251/4

H465/403
H2718
H3218
K251/4

32

(Stitches in photo are actual size.)

Supplies

2-mm seed beads:	H30, H40, H3766
1.6-mm Delica beads:	DB253, DB420
2.2-mm 3-cut beads:	H2781, H2782
6-mm bugle beads:	H69
2.5-mm triangle beads:	H3218, H3250
Pearl beads:	K251/3 (3mm), K251/4 (4mm)
Cupped sequins:	H468/402 (5mm), H465/403, H483/403, H486/403 (6mm), H488/404 (8mm)

Edgings

These look wonderful on cuffs and collars.

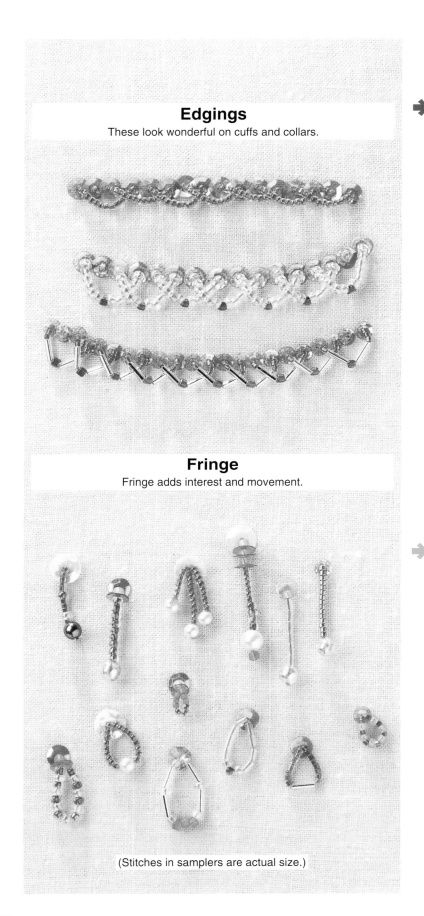

Fringe

Fringe adds interest and movement.

(Stitches in samplers are actual size.)

Edging

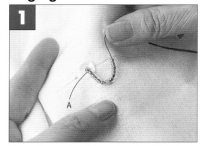

1

Bring thread out from back of fabric at A. Add sequin and beads.

4

It's easy to forget about the empty space one sequin wide at the starting point. Insert needle from wrong side of fabric, add a sequin and some beads, insert needle into sequin again and end.

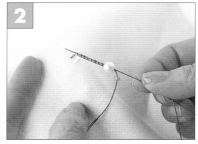

2

Except for the bead added last, run the needle back through the beads to the starting point.

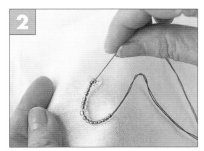

2

Pass needle through sequin again.

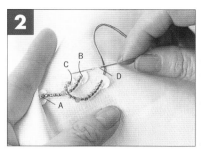

Continuing from (A) and leaving enough space for two sequins, insert needle at (B) and, following the outline stitch concept, go back the width of one sequin (C). Add the next sequin and beads. Leave enough space for one sequin, and insert needle into fabric at (D). Continue in the same way.

Note: Remember to leave space for two sequins at the beginning, and one sequin thereafter.

If you're stitching in a straight line, go back the width of one sequin, insert needle into fabric then make an ending knot.

Note: To make edging loops longer, add more beads.

Fringe

If you're working in the round (on a cuff, for instance), pass the needle under the first bead loop and then end.

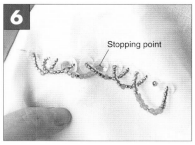

This is the stopping point for an edging made in the round.

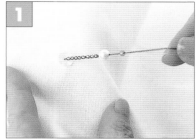

String the beads and sequins for fringe.

Looped fringe

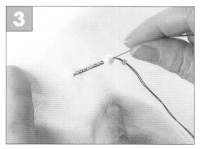

Pass needle through hole in sequin and bring it out on wrong side of fabric.

Pull thread and make a knot.

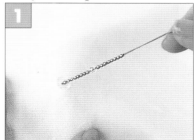

String beads for first loop.

Fringe with looped end

Pull thread.

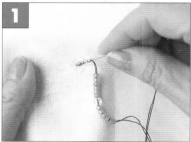

String beads, then run needle back through first beads strung (skipping beads in loop).

Now loop dangles from straight line of beads.

Raised stitches
Hidden beads add volume to these stitches.

Bead flower stitches
Stitches that give flowers movement and three-dimensionality

(Stitches in samplers are actual size.)

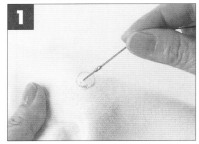

String several beads in center of pattern for the foundation.

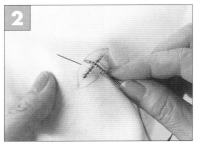

Use fewer beads for the left half of the circle than you did for the center.

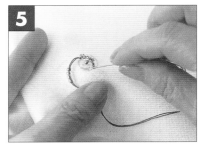

Work Satin Stitch A, beginning at center.

Continue making petals, vertical petals first, horizontal petals (if any) next, and then diagonal petals (if any), following the lines on your pattern.

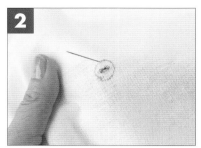

Bring needle out at edge of circle.

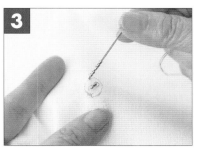

String more beads.

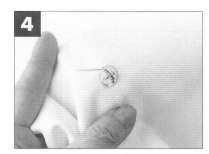

Add enough beads to form a vertical line across circle at center. Bring needle out right next to first bead added.

Raised oval

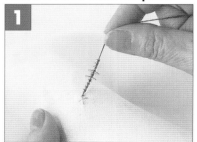

Bring needle out on opposite side.

Add the same number of beads for right half to complete circle.

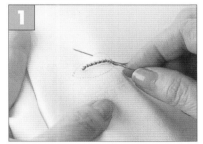

Make bead foundation.

Bead flower

Work one half, then the other.

Bring needle out on right side and add the beads for one petal.

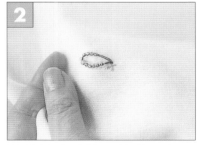

Insert needle right next to thread extending from fabric.

Bead flower with sequins

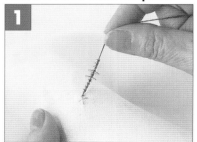

For best results, position sequins with their backs facing each other.

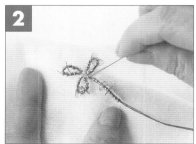

Use the same (bead flower) technique.

Sequin flower stitch
Combines sequins and beads for a three-dimensional look

Additional ideas
Use sequins of different shapes.

(Stitches in samplers are actual size.)

Sequin flower

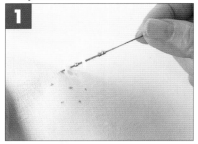

1

For the base of the flower, string beads between pairs of sequins.

5

Add a pearl bead at center of flower.

Variation on previous stitch

1

Try adding a few more beads between the sequins.

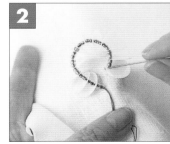

2

Form a circle.

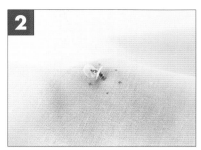

2

Work from the outside of petal toward the center.

3

Continue forming petals, using the same number of sequins and beads.

4

The sequins in the center, surrounded by beads, will stand up.

Adding dimension to sequins

1

Pass needle through a star-shaped sequin, a bead, then another sequin.

2

Work in the same way as fringe, running the needle back through all beads except for the last one strung.

3

When you pull the thread, you'll have a three-dimensional star.

2

Follow directions for raised star above.

3

With the additional beads, the flower looks even more three-dimensional.

Here are some more ideas:

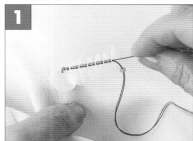

1

Alternate sequins and beads, using the fringe technique.

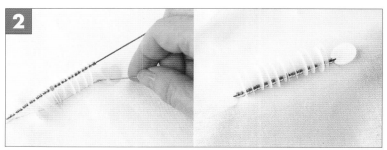

2

Or pull the thread tightly to form a horizontal row.

Cover Design
(Enlarge this 130%.)

When you're embroidering a large area (like
the sampler on the cover, for instance),
begin at the center and work toward the
edges. Work hanging or raised stitches next,
and detached stitches last of all.